Deep Space Discovery

EARTH AND OTHER INNER PLANETS

GAIL TERP

BLACK RABBIT BOOKS

Bolt is published by Black Rabbit Books
P.O. Box 227, Mankato, Minnesota, 56002.
www.blackrabbitbooks.com

Marysa Storm, editor; Grant Gould, designer;
Omay Ayres, photo researcher

Library of Congress Cataloging-in-Publication Data
Names: Terp, Gail, 1951- author.
Title: Earth and other inner planets / by Gail Terp.
Description: Mankato, Minnesota : Black Rabbit Books, [2019] | Series: Bolt. Deep space discovery | Audience: Ages 9-12. | Audience: Grades 4 to 6. | Includes bibliographical references and index.
Identifiers: LCCN 2017022132 (print) | LCCN 2017028458 (ebook) | ISBN 9781680725353 (ebook) | ISBN 9781680724196 (library binding) | ISBN 9781644662663 (paperback)
Subjects: LCSH: Inner planets–Juvenile literature. | Solar system–Juvenile literature.
Classification: LCC QB606 (ebook) | LCC QB606 .T47 2019 (print) | DDC 523.4-dc23
LC record available at https://lccn.loc.gov/2017022132

Image Credits

Alamy: Irina Dmitrienko, 27 (bttm r); iStock: inhauscreative, 31; esa.int/spaceinimages/Images: ESA, 25; mars.nasa.gov: NASA, 24 (bttm), 27 (top); nasa.gov: NASA, 5 (Earth), 24 (top), 26 (top l, bttm); nssdc.gsfc.nasa.gov: NASA/NSSDC, 27 (bttm l); Shutterstock: Alones, 28–29; Azuzl, 22–23 (planets, sun); Bobnevv, 23 (bttm r); cigdem, 9, 32; Filipe Frazao, 1, 16; gjebic nicolae, 26–27; Harvepino, 18–19; Hein Nouwens, 6–7; Johan Swanepoel, 18 (core); Jurik Peter, 20–21; Marc Ward, 19 (magnetic field); Maxal Tamor, 12; Mopic, 10–11; NASA images, 15; Nerthuz, Cover (space station); NikoNomad, 3; smartdesign91, 21 (arrows); Somchai Som, Cover (planet); Vadim Sadovski, 6, 21 (planet), 26 (top r); Yuriy Mazur, 23 (starry bkgd); spaceflight.nasa.gov: NASA, 4

CONTENTS

CHAPTER 1

Spectacular SPACE

In 1972, three astronauts went to the moon. As the men traveled, they looked down at Earth. They watched as the planet they called home got smaller and smaller.

From space, Earth looked blue with large white swirls. The blue was Earth's water. The white swirls were clouds. The astronauts saw huge landmasses too. The astronauts took a photo of their amazing planet.

Ancient people believed the sun and other planets orbited Earth.

The Solar System

Since ancient times, people have known about planets. They knew the planets weren't stars. The planets didn't move across the sky the same way stars did.

Later, people learned planets are huge bodies that orbit stars. Earth and seven other planets orbit the sun. The sun's **gravity** holds them in their paths. They make up the solar system.

Eight Planets

The four planets closest to the sun are the inner planets. Earth is one of them. The others are Mercury, Venus, and Mars. These planets have hard surfaces.

The planets farthest from the sun are the outer planets. They are made mostly of gas. They are big. People call them the gas giants.

From 1930 to 2006, there were nine planets. In 2006, scientists relabeled the ninth planet, Pluto, a dwarf planet.

outer planets

inner planets
Mars
Earth
Venus
Mercury

CHAPTER 2

The Inner PLANETS

Mercury is the closest planet to the sun. It is also the smallest. The planet has long cliffs. Some of them are hundreds of miles long. It's also covered with **craters**. Mercury has no **atmosphere**. Almost no gases surround the planet.

Mercury travels faster than any other planet. It speeds around the sun at about 31 miles (50 kilometers) per second.

Venus

Venus isn't the closest planet to the sun. But it is the hottest. Its atmosphere is thick. The gases hold in heat. Venus is also the brightest planet. Sunlight bounces off its clouds. It's one of the easiest planets to see from Earth. Thousands of volcanoes cover Venus. Scientists think some are active. They could erupt.

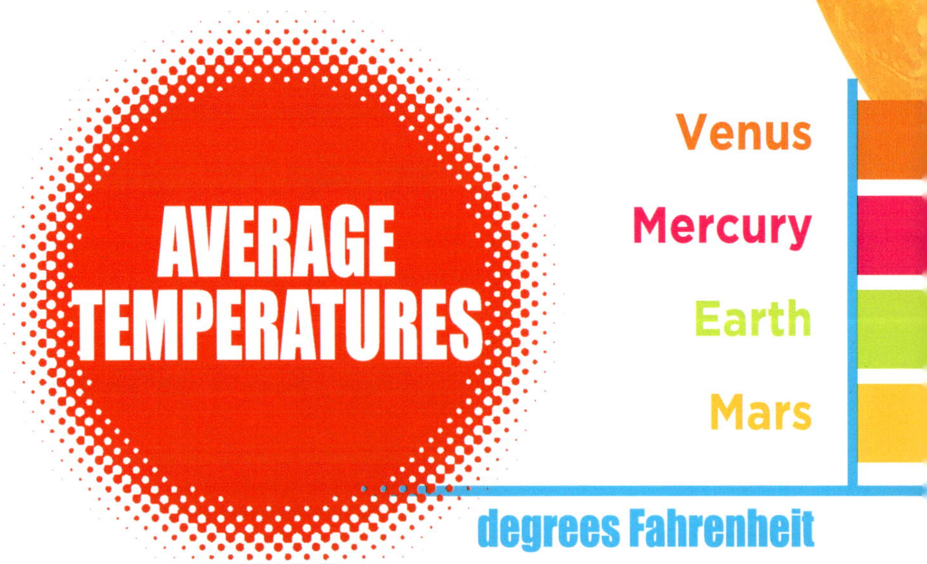

864 degrees Fahrenheit (462 degrees Celsius)
333 degrees Fahrenheit (167 degrees C)
60 degrees Fahrenheit (16 degrees C)
-80 degrees Fahrenheit (-62 degrees C)
-200
0
200
400
600
800
1,000

How Many Moons?

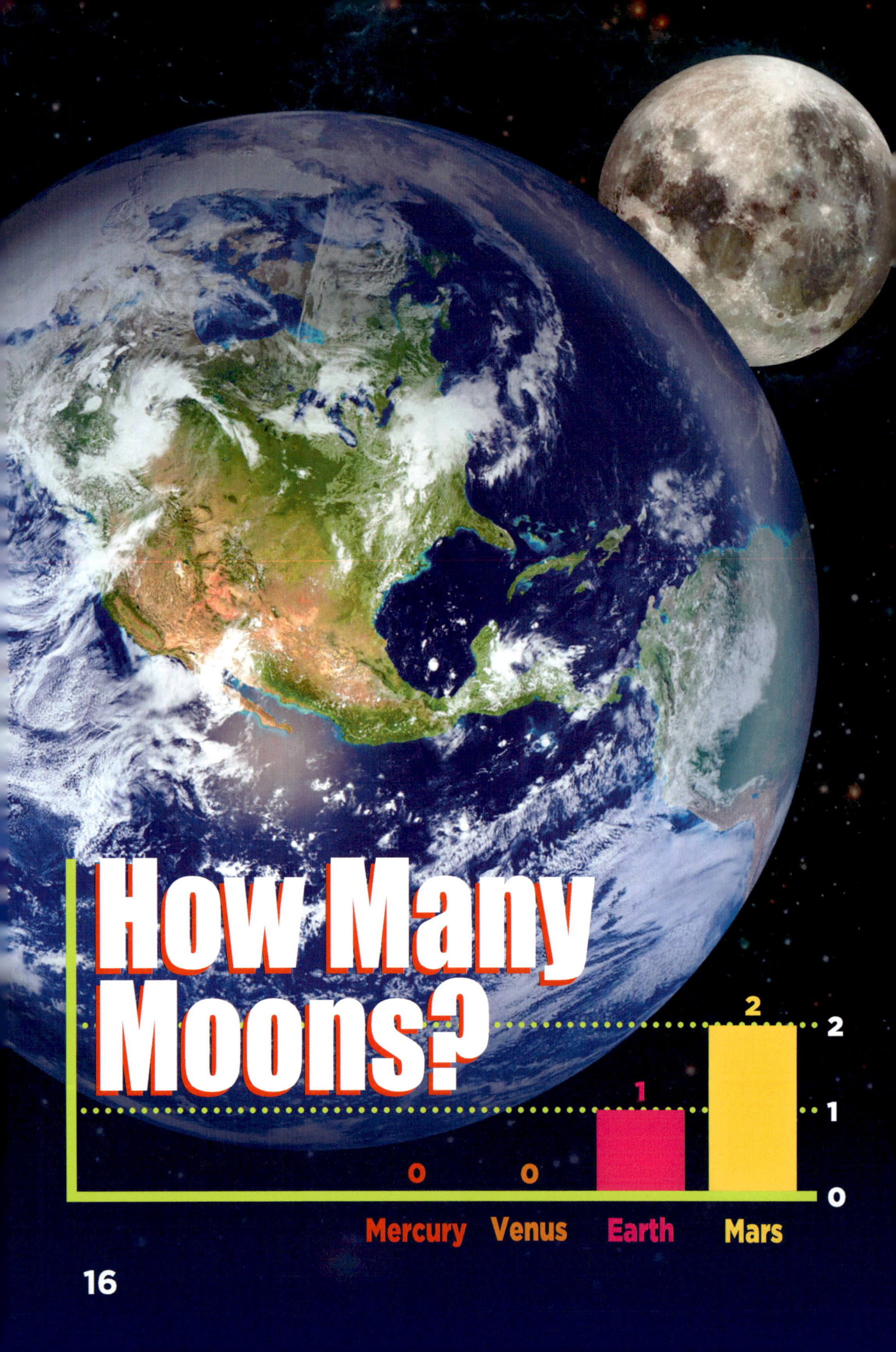

Earth

Earth is the largest inner planet. It's the only one with known life. One of the reasons Earth has life is its liquid water. In fact, water covers about 71 percent of its surface. Another reason Earth has life is its atmosphere. It's made up of **oxygen** and other gases. The atmosphere helps keep Earth's surface warm. It also protects Earth from the sun's harmful rays.

WHY DOES EARTH HAVE LIFE?

Earth has many features that help it support life.

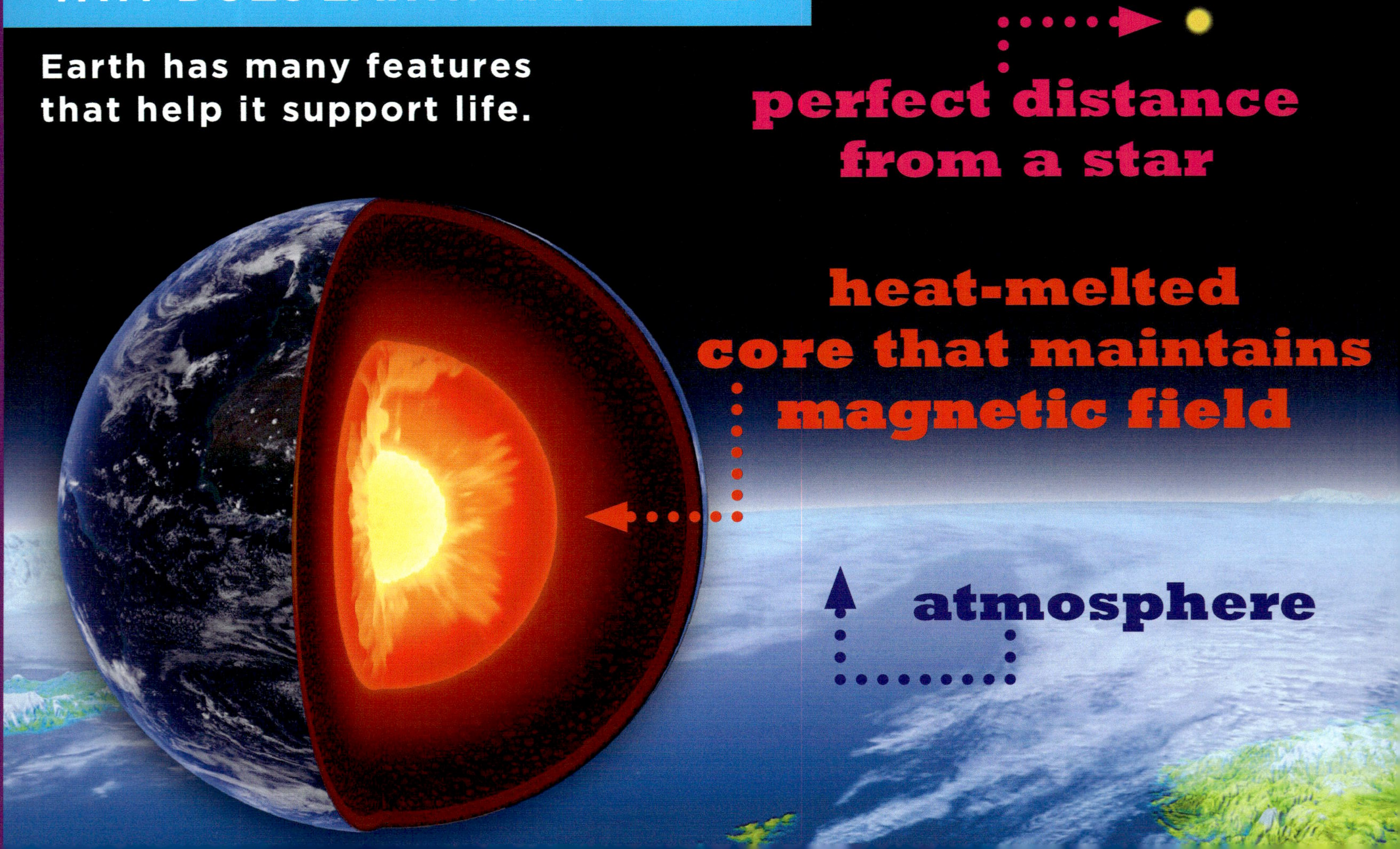

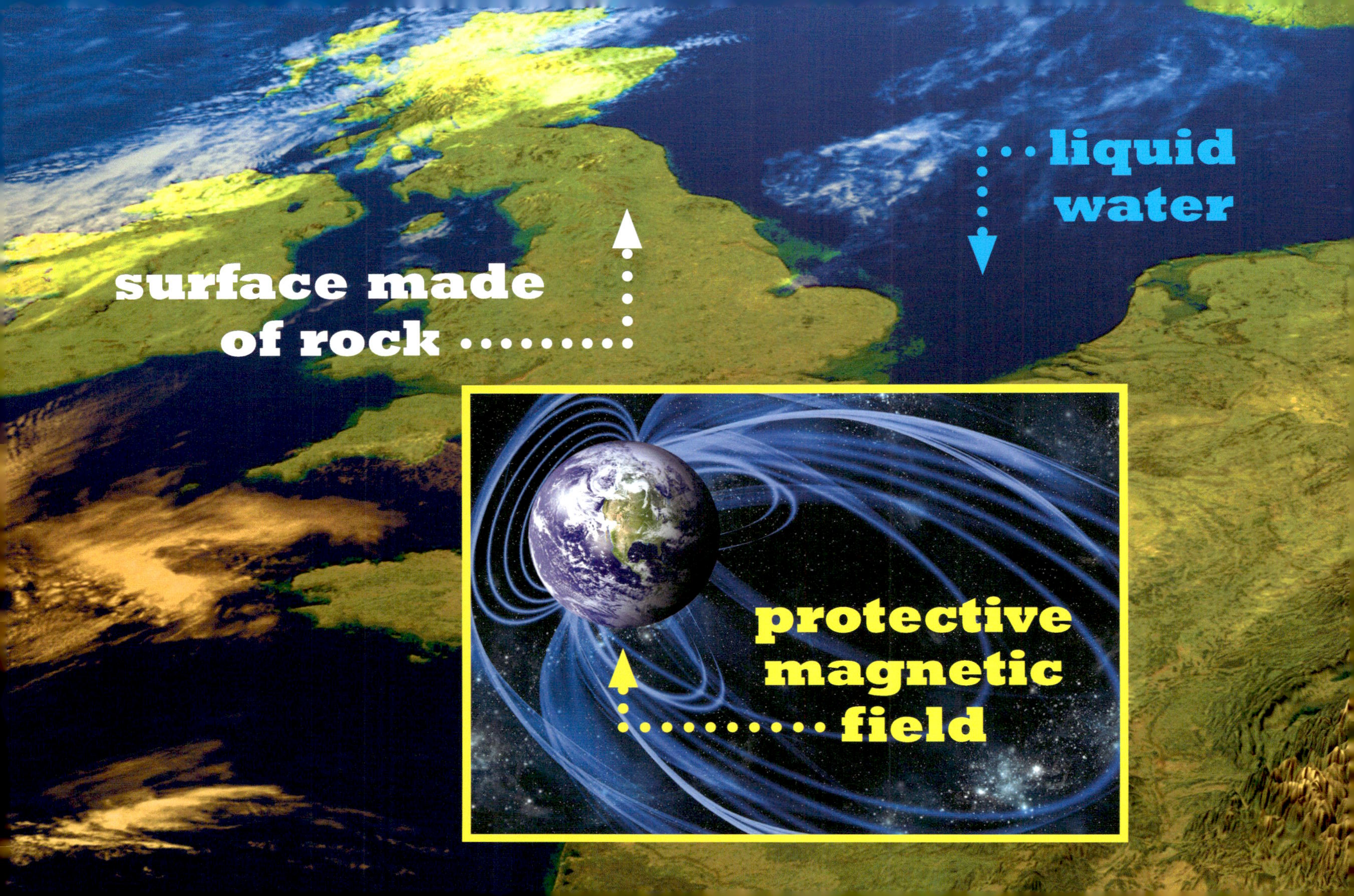
liquid water
surface made of rock
protective magnetic field

Mars

Mars is small. It's about half the size of Earth. Like Mercury, Mars has many craters. Mars has the largest volcano of all the planets.

Scientists think Mars once experienced huge floods. They would have happened billions of years ago. Water and flooding may be signs that Mars once had life.

A planet's day is how long it takes to spin around once. Some planets spin faster than others. They have shorter days.

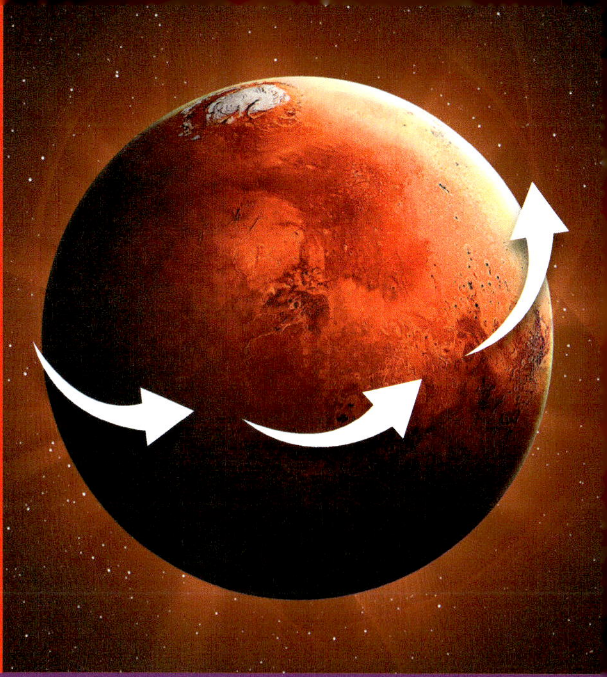

COMPARING THE INNER PLANETS

Diameter

Time to Orbit the Sun

687	Earth days	Mars
365	days	Earth
225	Earth days	Venus
88	Earth days	Mercury

LENGTH OF DAY

- **Venus** 5,832 Earth hours
- **Mercury** 1,416 Earth hours
- **Mars** 25 Earth hours
- **Earth** 24 hours

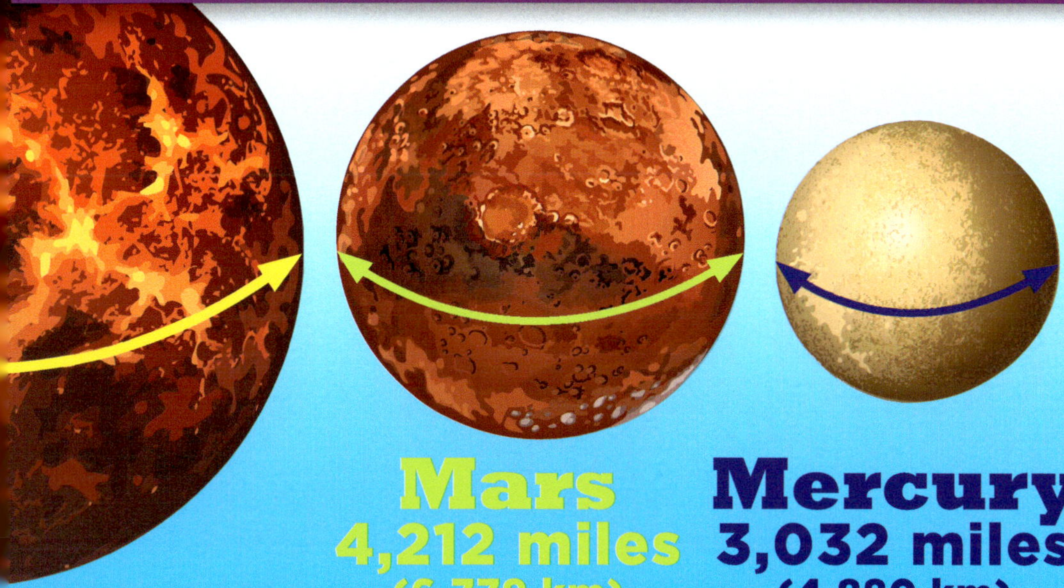

Mars
4,212 miles
(6,779 km)

Mercury
3,032 miles
(4,880 km)

AVERAGE DISTANCE FROM THE SUN

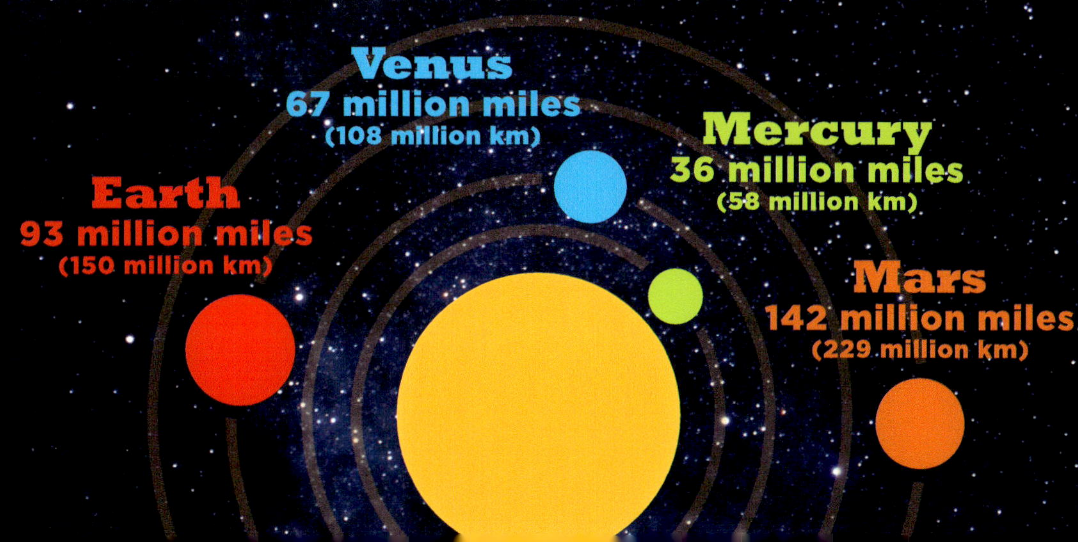

Missions to the Inner Planets

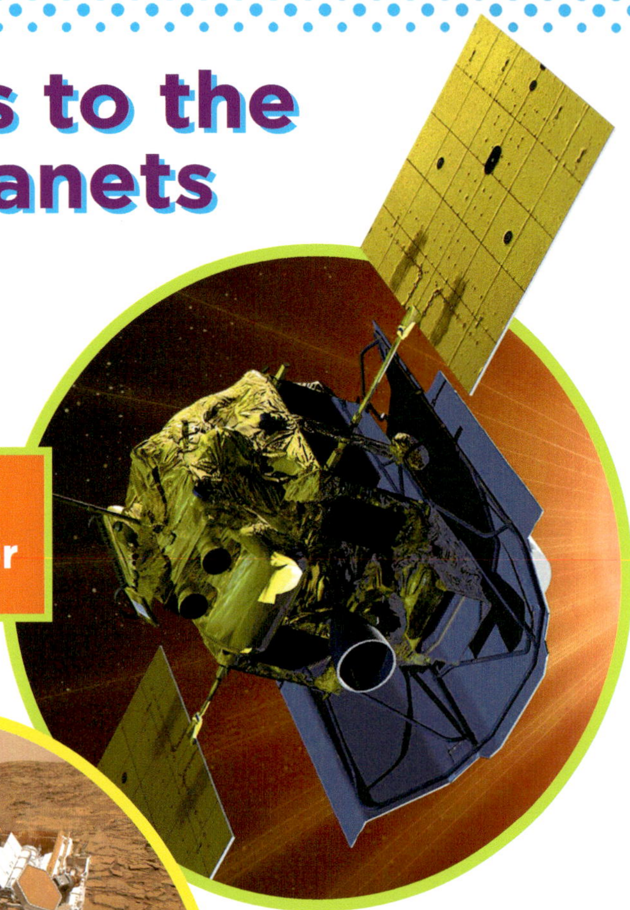

MESSENGER
Mercury orbiter

Curiosity
Mars rover

Venus Express
Venus orbiter

CHAPTER 3

Inner Planet EXPLORATION

In 1957, the first spacecraft circled Earth. Since then, there have been many missions to space. In the 1960s, **probes** reached Venus and Mars. In the 1970s, spacecraft flew by all of the inner planets.

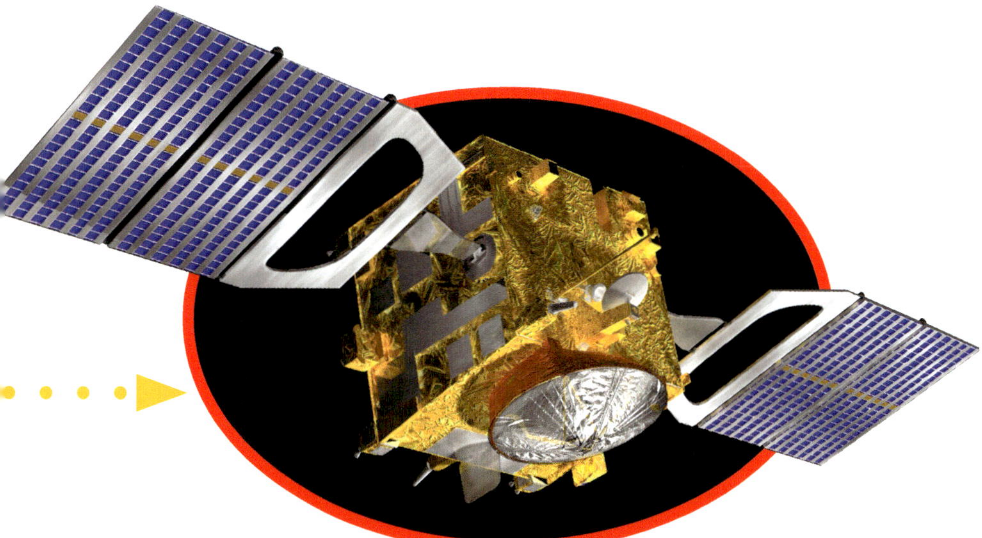

21ST CENTURY EXPLORATIONS

Many missions have gone to the inner planets since 2000. There have been many discoveries.

2002
Mission finds water ice on Mars.

2011
Mission to Mercury collects data and takes pictures.

2000

2005 to 2014
Spacecraft studies Venus' atmosphere and surface.

2012

A rover finds possible signs of life in Mars' past.

2020

2015

Spacecraft circles Venus.

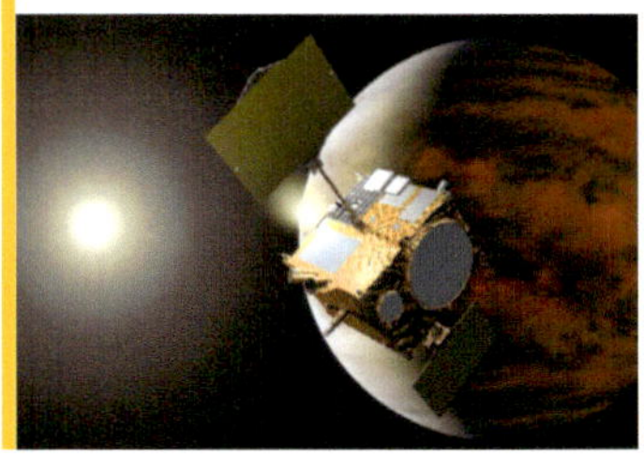

2016

Mission to find signs of life on Mars begins.

Future Explorations

There are big plans for more inner planet exploration. One plan is to send astronauts to Mars. This trip should happen in the 2030s. Until then, there is a lot of preparation to be done.

Space travel brings new knowledge. New information helps people learn about Earth and other planets.

ancient (AYN-shunt)—from a time long ago

atmosphere (AT-muhs-feer)—the gases that surround a planet

core (KOHR)—the central part of a planet or other body

crater (KREY-ter)—a hole formed by an impact

equator (ih-KWEY-ter)—an imaginary circle around Earth that is equally distant from the North Pole and the South Pole

gravity (GRAV-i-tee)—the natural force that pulls physical things toward each other

magnetic field (mag-NE-tik FEELD)—an area where an object's magnetic properties affect neighboring objects

orbit (AWR-bit)—the path taken by one body circling around another body

oxygen (AHK-si-jin)—a gas that is necessary for life

probe (PRHOB)—a device used to collect information from outer space and send it back to Earth

LEARN MORE

BOOKS

Dickmann, Nancy. *Exploring the Inner Planets.* Spectacular Space Science. New York: Rosen Publishing's Rosen Central, 2016.

Hamilton, Robert M. *Exploring Mercury.* Journey Through Our Solar System. New York: KidHaven Publishing, 2017.

Roumanis, Alexis. *Mars.* Meet the Planets. New York: Smartbook Media, Inc., 2018.

WEBSITES

Inner and Outer Planets
easyscienceforkids.com/inner-and-outer-planets/

Planet Earth
www.ducksters.com/science/earth.php

Solar System Facts
www.sciencekids.co.nz/sciencefacts/space/solarsystem.html

INDEX